D0717556

Acknowledgments

Alice Hoffman. From "It's a Wonderful House" by Alice Hoffman, first printed in *Architectural Digest*, December 1993. All rights reserved.

Joyce Carol Oates. From "Coming Home" by Joyce Carol Oates. Copyright © 1995 by The Ontario Review, Inc. Reprinted by permission of John Hawkins & Associates, Inc.

This book has been bound using handcraft methods, and is Smyth-sewn to ensure durability.

The cover and interior were illustrated by Barbara Strawser.

The dust jacket and interior were designed by Corinda J. Cook.

The text was edited by Tara Ann McFadden.

The text was set in Cochin.